Brown, to Brown

An Anthology by Danny Krivosh

WARNING!

EXPLICIT CONTENT, MAY TRIGGER
SOME READERS

Brown, to Brown

An Anthology by Danny Krivosh

Editing: Michaeli Translations

© All rights reserved to Danny Krivosh - 2024

No part of this book may be reproduced, copied, photocopied, recorded, translated, stored in a database, or transmitted in any manner or by any means, whether electronic, optical or mechanical (including photocopy, recording, Internet and e-mail) Commercial use of any kind of the content of this book is strictly prohibited without an authorization detailed in writing by the author.

simplestory
Digital Publishing

Contents

Welcome 5

A Name 11

Reflection 13

Wind, My Old Friend 16

Cancer 20

The Blue 22

Guillotine 25

Ana-Lisa 26

God Left Us (Homework) 31

No One's Land 33

Tale 43

Space Echo 47

Baker Street 50

Call Me Not 60

Shadow on the Hill 67

Safe Bets 78

Friend -- No Friend 81

Open House 83

A Single World 101

Wheels 103

Not to be 107

Welcome

My Pa could have –
my poem could have too, yet it did not,
'cause dying is what one could have done,
but as long as the could-haves contain certain would-haves,
some other better-suited ideas are to be condoned.

It's you, and it's time –
for a new poem.
No – too depressed to write a poem,
with all the could-haves and whatnots.
Press load to load the loading screen.
Press space to squeeze whatever time's caught between.
And now it's loading... yet again...

Guess we'll have to start over,
perhaps with a premium unlocked version,
with a privately-owned corpse that was modded extra-dirty.

This, and that, and pick a death for her –
Sorry! A path,
and ass and tits – fine teen galore.
Now that you've drowned her,
you're needed once more on shore.

Insignificance –
cracks appear on unsuspecting surfaces –
We're here to build apart together,
on an evening such as this –
Destined to turn out like many, many others,
this time it'll be –
on the lookouts – see?

Alone – and better off like it.
Things flying by –
Indeed, I am so high that
I can see things flying by,
but there's no way
that that's actual reality.
Not because I cannot see,
not because it would not happen,
just because I am,
and therefore – I guess.

Something must happen in this 'in-between'.
I'll wait – I don't mind the wait.
In this life as well as the other –
I will bring cookies for all haters and rapists,
just take a number and grab a seat.
Ouch, don't bite the hand that feeds.
Before one draws the final draw, I clamp up.
Shades under a curtain,
Looking in – who?
Whisper now: 'What do they see?'

Danny Krivosh

A very certain sort of curtain,
Dark vanilla, brown as sugar – sugar frost,
a laptop tossed from a room to a porch –
then all the way down to the pavement.
It would cry if it could.
It looks like it does.

Unmending little droplets of culture –
dripping down,
I like the sound, but it's forbidden.
So is torture,
Recalculated rapture for the living,
growing rapidly until it's punctured – yum.

Shit, I just can't help myself.
I am a product of the dying of the ages.
Livid in a cave where I'm okay for now,
but not for long.

From vinyl to being considered new,
to becoming vintage again only to be tossed away
like dirt.
Too filthy to be considered an emblem,
but it's still somewhere there – yes, still –
somewhere, alone, underappreciated and pure.
Pa's voice is faintly heard in the background,
like a good ol' prayer.

Somewhere, still feeling like some sort of a whole.
Still in that liminal cave,
A single whole – or so it seems –
is wreaking havoc upon the restless living.
Knees to the brink.
A new kind of kick.
A fetish,
a kink.
A look across the room –
a wink.
Repulsive,
I vomit all over my precious shoes.

Rapture!
Hear my angels roar in sullen angst,
Wailing at you as they commit suicide in your distasteful name.
Can you tell heavenly tears from incredible fury?
Can tears of fallen angels blow out the rings of fire?
Abhor the roar of my angels.

The shore ahead does lie.
When all signs and waves come crashing down to form a miserable-looking whole –
again...
You will rise.
Again...
But that's not the case for me – no, siree.
I've had enough, you see.

I will drop right here (stop the bus!) because I can,
and it's not a single life too soon.

Is it alive?
Shall we call a doctor?
Oh wait, never mind.
It's dead now.
Seems totally unimportant now, doesn't it?
Save me not.

The road ended right there –
at least as far as anyone living could tell.
To describe it?
Juicy, bouncy –
the road.
Yes, the road.
Filled with insects that come and bite you in the ass.
Annoying.
Perfect.
I'm just a boy again,
ready to get fucked by a stranger in a gas station.
Welcome home, young man – old soul.
Willing to get fucked? Raped?
How 'bout a package deal?
We got you.
We do.
Choose how to get fucked.

Are you an actor?
Are you a teen?

Don't answer that unless you are ready
To be a man,
to be mean to the other girls in order to get to where you want,
Win yourself a spot among the other drooling men.

The one I wanna sleep with is...
Not you.
Tears.
Match a tie around that neck –
tighten it so it'll feel just right,
nice and tight.
Again!

I am an unprotected marvelous little marble.
My Pa did not leave me tonight.
In a way
The way of the flash –
I think I was always on my own.
Don't you?

A Name

Sad as a motherfucking nightmare.
Hope to never see you again.
Into this another, here I go about without my man.
Taking me forever,
I don't know if I bother.
Signing in for later, who is who and how the hell have you been?

It's late at times, this I well know.
Sometimes I feel too well.
But how you've changed, how you've been gone.
How light has turned itself.
Silently in you, a spark to wit I'll hold my own.
Solemnly asleep with you, the man does die alone.

I cannot stress the weak parts of that same forgotten dream.
How you have turned around me, to make it seem like me.
It's good to be a coward.
I'd like you to agree.
This is the time for sorrow,
not what's under me.

It is a time for reading, for reflecting on a past.
Recollections call for this: The past to be the last.
A longer time does ask me to return, to be the man.

I'll spit for this, I'll scream for that, until we meet again.

It's been since you've met me.
A time you used to call me by a name.
Heard it from a stranger and now it's all there is – a name.
You'll get to where you want me, this I know too well.
A scene where you will try to speak a while before you fail.

Living is a frame and it will die within one man.
To bleed together, blend together, joined under a name.
Tell me of what makes you,
Not what makes you feel.
Say this one begets you.
Listen, don't reveal.
If it is your will, I'll sign –
if a man is what you need,
I'll breathe with you, I'll lie to you, I'll live with you.
I'll let you hurt me where my beauty slowly fades.

A chatroom filled with strangers, modernized, weaponized.
Said to last forever, maybe it can sink so low.
Burning lasts forever, not that I would know.

Reflection

There was a world for two, where the earth could only hold one. Through endless battles, the strong one made a strong case of winning, and as he kept his tears behind curtains, he made it so that the worst would always seal the deal – the very last King of Spades is what this is. But when his lies finally caught up with his shenanigans, he noticed how much less he cared now about everything and everyone, which, rest assured, would mean his defeat – this well he knew, and feared. Reflecting back from the monument of victory that's been a buffer – a constant reminder of the two opposing personas he held so dear – he came to grips with exactly what he needed to do to in order to win.
Too bad he was interrupted in medias res—
"You're the best salesperson I've ever met," said the weak one to his king. With pale skin and a shock that was real, he added: "I can see right through you."
I said: "Kindly, respectfully." Yes, I began building up my response: "I dismiss your allegations – for I have fought for us, and won, so it cannot get any more real than that, am I right? I am on your team, am I not?! What more do you fucking want from me?!!"
"Hold it right there," he said without flinching, without letting my vulgarity run wild inside him.

And so that was the moment I knew he was on to me. "You've only fought for you, and no one else," he said, and after that, rather clumsily, he fell upon receiving a gentle blow, a caress really, in the shape of a fist right in the kisser. "Here, pick it up, you trash."
I turned my back on the weak puddle of mud in slo-mo, and the match did seem to have his one ideas. He dropped to the ground with his mouth opened wide, and I knew I done fucked up.
"Finally! The world shall be mine."
Alas – the weak one got up, and managed to place his slimy hands all over my precious spirit, locked it, and threw away what mattered most – a key.
In a white room where I am currently held against my will, I am tied to the toilet – no less. "Open up! Let me out! It's not fucking funny!" All I'm left now is a white room, where a past I will never return to dies slowly – evaporating in all the white, and so I am a visitor of my own reflection in the only mirror I could find – and it's in my memory, nowhere else; a past with a gruesome ending reflecting back from a past self in front of a magical chrome bean – that's what it all comes down to; it is that gorgeous chrome bean of a foggy city I used to call 'my home.' Watching my own steps revisit the winds of an evasive memory – the world was mine and is no longer. Bring me back to thee!
No, you're not going back –
You're good right here.

But I need it so – why can't I have it? It used to be all mine for ages before the undertaking – the shelves of human experience were mine before the ugly world war came a-crashing down over my dreamworld, taking everything and everyone.

There emerged a puddle of blood, and I moaned as I drank from that nectar of the gods.

It smelled of man with his tail tucked in.

"This paradise belongs to me now."

Wind, My Old Friend

I wrote it when it mattered.
Not long after that, not when the tables turned.

The vein popped.
The sugar cube quickly dissolved in fear, leaving only the stick standing
On its own against the violent shadows of the tallest groves.
That's when the twitching started.

Never lose your way!
You hear me, you imbecile? One.
It's the one you came in from, you good-for-nothing idiot! One, Two.
Get it? Got that in that stupid little head of yours? Now go on!
Get the hell outta my sight.

No wonder, I wonder –
that the wind's embrace felt so much nicer after that,
better than anything I ever had the misery of knowing up to that point.
I loved you at times, especially at first when you were so cool –
came so swiftly and left in that same rush.

I also respected you when you stopped, but I never, ever let you leave my sight.

What was that?
Take it all the way back and keep it shut!
Wouldn't carry the distance anyhow...
"What?"
I said I'll leave this one for you to finish!
Now get the hell outta my sight, you... you...
You bunch of morons!!

God. Alright, let's dive back in and cross worlds or whatever the fuck I was about to...
"What? What did you say? We... we can't hear you! What's... do you know this guy?"

Stop muttering, you babbling moron.
One, Two, and Three.
My jawbone got unhinged from laughing too hard.
Had enough, perhaps.
No, he's... just freshening up.
He'll be right back.

That was the moment I decided to finally stop my foolishness once and for all,
but I shouldn't have been so quick to set the stage.
I should have looked for wherever I'd come in from instead.

Yet there it was.
A busted, uninviting, soon-to-be-discovered room.
Ah, shit, I missed it!
The drapes, they moved a bit!
They had not the decency to admit,
and of course the mattress wouldn't say anything –
being the counter's bitch and all –
but… I know…

The room got trashed to bits.
Three covered walls, an edge of a twin bed on top
of which are my worthless limbs, and –
out front is an infuriatingly mundane-looking
counter, undeservingly given center stage.
A scraping, good-for-nothing counter piece of shit.
Work, work, work, and after a while you're done
for.
That means you'll never have to work again!
That hard and nasty nail attracts my attention.
How it clings to the wood, as I would never have
the balls to do.
He never wanted anything from you or anyone!
"How dare you speak your mind?!"
I spank the empty holster.
"Now get outta my sight, you goddamn babbling
moron."
With that flip of a hand, I turn in.

At a grave distance, a final return reveals no witnesses.
The wind hits hard on the counter's side.
It's always at the loudest when I burst into uncontrollable laughter.
Took me a while to calm myself down from that one.
Then I kept on laughing... quietly, defiantly, but expressively enough
for that son of a bitch to know that I...
Yes, I – have the higher ground.

Cancer

I let them
brainwash me,
wash me sprinkly-clean –
I like crack.
I'll fight this ghastly wind with my bare and
broken arms –
nothing more.

Move – I tell you!
Fly, hot darn it!
From watered toes to smoke and mirrors,
I wish you'd tighten your shoelaces – I mean, it's
only been forever.
Spring chicken-crisp, dirty gauntlets of fire –
blasphemous desire.

Crack – there goes my skin –
Crack – o' how the mighty have shrunken in,
from a great height and into this shithole.

Void of tears, they cry out – "Why?" well, why the
fuck not?
Hardly alive, they tread the universe like specks of
dust,
reaching where the horizon has just missed its date.
She was always a slut and we all know it, Horizon.
It's okay, homie, we got you.
Let's. Go. Home.

Little blue school scouts looking up high to Mr. No-Good up in the sky,
called heaven now but the unreachable suits it best.
The slut's heels are as high and mighty as a devotee.
Clunky skull heads, they go into the fire of concepts unnerved, unveiled.

Smoking.
You know?
Just – chillin' in the morning bliss, alright?
Fuck! A bright light blinds my eyes shut and I mourn.
Feeling silly with my six pack of –
Dead, I sink into a smothering and hazy morning, and forget –
just quite forget of all the –
Of all that I somehow managed to slip into a –
Now I'll have to make something up just to make it up.

(Hey that's a joke I could have made!)

A man passed me by to pass through to the water gate.
His lifted eyes looked straight at me like a six-pack of wrongs to make me quite right.
Exalted, I slipped in and rejoiced.

The Blue

The sun shone in a lively manner, but it shouldn't have.
The blue came out of its transmission vehicle.
It heavily evaporated in dismissal of my ability to stand comfortably on the sidewalk.
"State your business," demanded the man in uniform –
looking for another textbook response in his day full of common bullshit.
"Fuck if I know, I'm just me," I quickly replied. Too quickly.
He noticed my lack of care.
Something weird started building right there.
"Watch your French, mister, or I will have to do something about that dirty mouth of yours."
He got offended by my immaturity, and nothing seemed to matter anymore.
My mouth watered, but it's gonna dry before dark, this I well know.
Could I have said it any other way? Honestly – fuck if I know.
Too bad, I thought, in a final moment mixed with stupidity and happiness, I was only just beginning my fit.
Evil, sexy, I scratched the inside of my pockets, where I found my cock,
and I started gently caressing it through the fiber.

Found it! I put on a dirty smile of satisfaction.
Was it for him to see?
My eyes found the sky.
Blissful in that very moment, I regained my manhood for a sharp second.
Just enough to say:
"Hey, fuck you," and I actually meant it.
"What did you just say?" He took two steps forward, menacing whatever I had left installed.
On the third step, he done reached for it and said: "I did warn you there would be consequences."
"Why didn't you listen? Hey! Stop! Hey!"
He pulled me out of my elements. I didn't even notice I was backing off.
"What!" he shouted without even asking a question, but it did get his point across.
"I mean," he tried to reason with me, "do you... do you think it's easy for me?"
He didn't stop there. Nope...
He continued spiraling down into that common frenzy.
Too common for that everyday business.
And then, an explosion – allowed by all rights of guilt-free conscience – hit me.
He's powerful.
He knows it.
He's backed by some kind of honorable law that allows him to do me right here.
A fourth step and a slightly different approach from the uniformed mouth:

"Do you have trouble hearing me, mister?"
He didn't ask me a question here either, for if he did, I would have known the answer.
I'm fucked, I thought to my poor self...
His eyes widened, and among all the blue, red turned green:
"Turn the fuck around, you piece of shit."
I wanted to switch roles for just a moment, and tell him:
"Blah blah blah! Consequences shmosequences!"
But I didn't.
Somewhat amused by that dumb thought, I turned around and dropped my pants.

The shy sun seemed to notice, for it started its daily decline right then, which was a little too early, and a cloud had cast a shadow on the sinful city that is my hometown.
I was born here. Raised to perfection.
Fuck me, I thought, this will be it for me.
"I'm done! Come get me!"
A tear and smile, with my pants off – this is me.
"Fuck me." I spluttered into thin air with my back to authority,
hoping it would catch my crude invitation through the void between us.
"Break me, kind sir, for I need to understand your power better."

Guillotine

This is some end.
Lips – smear one on it.
Hips tear and wear.

You are the one out the door.
Could you have sunk any lower?
Time will break away, secretly.
Seek-cred, ill-will – ye half-strung Guillotine.

You're as impressive as a massive stroke –
why is that mine?

Broke, woke –
prep me.

Protocol – got 'got'.
Got gotten.
She'll smear my smiling lips unto thine collar,
trap my strap-on.

You do own
me and I do all for your enjoyment –
my entrapment.

Everyone –
is you.
Everyone –
is less than me except for my Guillotine.

I merely miss you, and that is all.

Ana-Lisa

Part I

Who am I?
Tied-end fried,
Roughed up, roughly milled yet unrecognizable by these o'–so-many miles of 'no one sees me' –
I can see me.
I spot the womb.
Sturdy, the kiss rises henceforth, and the rose thus covers and diminishes within a lost raider's ark.
Sit back down, slut.
Know anything I don't, or is it the "I" that bounds and deceives the very core of a curator's verse?
Detain her.
Lay everything down.
Upraise –
Do what old Daddy says –
kill the mayor, and all of your neighbors – throw in a ditch.
Stay all the way away and do as I say, for it is the day's command.
So, who am the "I"?
Intonation breaks my merry heart's obtainable peace.
My Mary and I shall carry the pieces forward.

Part II

Hold it a while before you frisk me, and drink what is rightfully mine, kind sir.
Lower your stare and beseech, preach, finch –
teach my system how to rise again, and perhaps withstand –
become immune to upgrades of any unsavory cause or mishap.
It is skill – not chance that binds us, dear sir.
May the de-void be, for once, and as I raise a glass to all who were to be condemned from the very beginning, I ask with a slow sigh:
May you all die; may the widths of your previous so-called achievements run out and be pulled off the stem, one lousy pixeled clue at a time, so –
Who am I?
The resolution indubitably entails us with an end-plan –
So that, little by little, disgust and mistrust can become the cheesy crust of the surface,
so that a forceful re-entry into a poor man's heart's infrastructure may become feasible.

I really don't need this dance routine.
I swing by the man I could have indulged myself in being and await my wholeness.
My little come-between comes out, and by 'out' I mean it invades your privacy, and you take a giant leap back.

This is a little of a little of me, and my off-boat sure seems like I caught wind in a dream and married a soothsayer.
A little –
Sing into my upper mouth, and I'll keep on keepin' something still.

Part III

Without widows, windows or cement, I take her desire to be broken as a joke that will now accompany me on my fairly-long journey to the tomb.
I take, flip and keep a little of her misbehavior with me forever, and it cheers my angry, oh-so-extremely powerful and angry punctured glass armor.
Tore it.
It itted, tilted, tried to cry and forgot the 'why' of it all.
Had to stop it with another sudden blow.
Knew I had to do her right, so I held her tight, and the "you know it will be alright" came out.
And it will! – more so now than ever.
I try her every dime and tire her in doing so.
I tighten the screw of her flat tire, and cry for the moon of her elapsing wisdom.
The night answers my prayer, but I am already past the dam in front of the telly.
I come a-faucet into her, and the paradigm shifts.
The smoke clears and the tale springs on.
Done (for the night).

A tear in the fabric of the earth hurts us all, like a blow which is a ricochet of our libidinal discourse.
Curiosity comes free, and it looms in the toppings of our hearts,
while the carton box gets reused without ever revealing a hint of sorrow on its wrinkled behalf –
while they all see, know and condemn.
They lower their expectations because they know the performer well enough, and the stage thus becomes a tool, where we manage to triumph over wrongful misdoings, imaginations, presumptions, as well as pre-emptive assumptions.
Most kids throw themselves at others – they have never even heard of a 'dream-come-true', and that boggles their simple minds.
Buggers by the lot they are, I kid you not.
The sinner's light is sinister, and the
Mosquito had no reason to break me, but bite it did, the tiny fellow.
As such – a cross has had to be carried every Thursday since,
to pay for protection, respects.
Right, Left,
Right, and so on.
I lent a knee and crossed the dimension of 3 crosses standing tall,
Absolutely killing me with their struggle to identify as more.
I shrink in this pathetic existence, and cry for their forgiveness, but my attempt falters.

Part IV

To whom I may matter, yonder is the where –
you'll go to my grave.
Still –
I'm fairly consistent with the amount of shit I've twelve-yeared.
You're on. (We're on...)
You are none, and –
we are trophies.
The trumpet sends a trope to all toppings, and they sweeten their grasp in return, on account of the crunchy old surface resembling the earth on top of which they stand, seek protection,
Respects.
The crust befalls all visitors and onlookers, but not before claiming the lives of some suitors.
I would like a visitor, but how can I get someone to care for me if I never dared foster a fire with the blameful drops of caramel?
I happened to have used spice time and thyme again,
till my balls dropped.
That time I was caught off-guard, I know, but be not alarmed – I am still my own.
Still –
Rejoice, o you.
Yours, your yes as well as my Yellowstone –
Yearn.
Flower!
Buns of tasteful good-riddance.

God Left Us (Homework)

God on two legs has six.
Humans never stood a chance,
nor do they participate as audiences of their own
free will as they lay it on:
Being alive, it's called, and it'll broadcast on all
channels except the one that matters to you.
There, I've said it: my heart aches.
Strong winds, fuck you.
Five lack the skill while the other two jive.
Deep down they dive, no reason to cry for school,
mention, forget, interiors collapse the whole,
am I the only fool left on this godforsaken land, or
something of that sort?
Fuck you.
Man.
Smelly.
So be it.
God be with.
You –
a look out the window and all I see is –
Fools know me, stable sharpeners seem to roll off
me as the land becomes me and I pee.
My hair, my sprawling skin is in
all of them.
Their daughters restrict me from being free, that's
you.
My human, my –

fucking naked individual.
Far is the non-idle from your soul.
Dancers of all alike, and this here too.
Oh, and that;
Let that be all that will forever break my soul into a morbid forever behind a smoke screen of –
more than forever to uphold that marrow bone.

God riddle.
Good riddle.
God riddance.
God faithful.
And more.
And ever.
And none come between us, we'll get her –
The Mother;
the incomprehensible night light mire.
What – where?
Nightmare.
Hope you will find her deep inside you – you know –
where no one dared to crawl…?
–ever?

No One's Land

There is a haven of provision under the sun.
The same does not apply for the emptiness in me.
A simple, albeit not altogether-grounded notion –
Triumphed over the opposition, as if there was
anything to fear.

Adaptation can become the curve through which
direct opposition may
apply force — on the main pipeline which is not
unlike a father.
About my acrylic mother, I'd say she is an energy
faucet.

I hide like a bird in my cage.
The bars answer to none but the golden lock —
obviously. It may one day cave for the one who is a
non-at-all.
But 'non-at-alls' matter —
As they mount up a steed, they multiply, bump
headfirst into the entrance steadfast.
The ballroom is about to begin on the groundless
turf.
A saddle should never have, twice or thrice before,
but it did, and who'd tell it not to?
This is the now, where the emptiness confesses,
undresses, SS's, and all the while – the 'no-one's
silhouettes spin out of control.

Ay, yes – the wooden dream team of forgotten promises...
And the day goes on, and on, uplifts, turns fits, and on, almost dying from belonging to a numerical figure that is to none.
No... none at all.
No —
Just that – resembling of a thing. Yes —
What a shrinkly bobblehead it had, and a face held by the hopeless shapelessness of mankind.
What I staple to is what I truly trace – me.

A week later

I still hide in my cave... can't leave here – my miserable little playground seems to attract much-unneeded attention. They come in graves, the meat-growers, the water-fighters, the still collaborators of insanity as well as of vanity.
In it, one must dare to believe before he behaves.

It behooves one, so it says on the box.
That runway choice asks me to –
Mimic, to be of something only to –
Gaze, you miserable sorrowful earthling;
Incompetent jazz listener, dance!

Why at all, on the floor, if it never even evened?
Not at all, not even a bit —
Not a second to be content –
hand it over.

Not a beat, not a slick, not that I care –
Over –
there is not a single concern in my heart, the fire
of which has just burned out.
Never –
not a no, not a 'let us forget why the whys ever
entered my house of seclusion in the first place'.

There is not one, but many a 'hell no's',
sitting on a bench, listening to the news,
grinning — teeth.
Fateful is a joke song – full worth, careful –
as not to spill.
Do not spoil the remains. Some people eat that shit.

A month passes

A sitting throne gets laughed at by the kindle that
was wrongly delivered to an angry stiff lip, and to
him alone, he seems concerned (he's a fucking liar).
He'll forgive all that ever was, but until he does,
he'll
bow to no one – he won't believe until he feels the
foot.
It behooves him still, there under, in his idea of
hell.

"Do not return empty-handed.
Bring it home, home-run,
home-boy, and run my errands,
FOR ME!

Go to the market by the den of the Sundance
festival, and breathe the same air as I —
into the cash, register your hands.
They might falter, but you'll take it!
All of it!
By the will of some odd man, by the deeds of 'no
fair' bazaar, by the mask of integrity and all that is
seemingly worth it, you will get it done."

By the forceful day's end, the call comes through:
'Here comes, here he comes — and there he is!'
The man does come alone, in his shiny armor.
He is masked so as not to cry, not to beg, not to be
little.
Then he stumbles all wrong and in an instant
becomes a none-at-all.
As he lingers on, wishing for another cheekbone
(yet again...)
the sea stalls.

The day goes on and on, and the wildflowers grow
old by the lair of the banished,
and I don't care.
I know something they don't.
I see them for what they truly are.
They crumble at the sight of a light in the sky, like
the one from the Neverending Story, which was
my brief life on a shelf, to be discarded, disavowed,
untitled and un-tilted.

A simple question can throw itself into the air, so
believes the 'I' in me.
The skillful draws near a figure skater out of a
picture that is a poor reminder of a blasting past
— and no-one's coming... fast.
By whomever's words mean to be meant, there is a
word of choice, and the
one commands. There is an army under him,
in a river of demolition.
A pile of little somethings —
They are so cute.
They are to die for, and just like the muzzle, they
cover yours truly.

Devotion is not to a note, and yet you stick and
push and play like your life deserves it.
To be okay,
to be the moron –
to never dare walk away.
To age is to long, to mislead,
to drill deep into an electronic feed. It is just it, and
it is all that it forever will be.
If we're lucky,
It'll end abruptly on a day without a note.
We'll breathe our last breaths.
It'll create the sense of pre-tense, that nothing is
the matter anymore,
that no one needs a father,
and thus create the one true mother —
of All.

Brown to Brown

It was a rainy day in No-One's Land.
A little seed became a slight remnant of a verse.
A simple type of question went unanswered, and
the false inclusion
included hers. She set sail to no avail,
into some gotten-odd
forgotten tale. I greet her at
the door and forget.

As she weaves her empty charm, she drifts away
from reason's calm.
She takes her leave after her mother's tension.
She tries to dance, but I can sense
that there is nothing else in the promised land of
fools.
Some moment's nigh. (Sigh.)
Of no one's pain and nomad's misery and
god's disdain, I shrink like the pain that
went way under.
Of showering rains, of little to nothing
— of unmarked stains,
I come to listen to nothing —
And oh, how it comes in plenty a rhyme and
chance.

A marble.
A breakable pact,
and as a matter of fact,
I try but no one hears,
since no one fears,

and though I manage to come near,
I never know exactly what it was that I used to hear.
I forget.

I used to care because I used to use. I used to pray.
I used to ask you what's with the fake tears — so
now... what's with the —
I don't care now.
Do Not widen your touring eyes.
Do not even ask me if I have you in my thoughts
or something else in mind.
I only write to you about this, which is nothing.
I do all which is nothing, and something in you
wants some more.

But no, you see —
I can't, and won't ever dye the
store. I'm back here now,
floor...
And that's a song —
of that I'm sure,
As well as of my love.
Of all that this is for, I sing along,
yet sing alone,
for you are not with me.
From afar, I just adore.
I abhor past revisits.

Nowadays

I just abort and consolidate, I come in late,
And our time was never ours to begin with.

Dreams and whims of sunlight fly around me.
My heavy, conscious head weighs down the path of contortion.
More contour, not texture, please — not for her,
Not –
With –

Time.
Time and time and waistlines, and smell, and yet again –
another creature.
Another question, and to answer yours — I am to befriend
the angel of darkness —
Not floors!

Ah, yes, of course!
I'll bring you
nothing,
For there is nothing in the rain that tells lies —
these are but signs that
appear from nowhere, to make me cry a tad, only to finally go away.

All in all, we are at that pathway, but it seems
unlike one. The hallmark evaporates into a channel
for the sweet indoors.
Now the deep implores —
"Sweep the floors! Make me even, even if you
cannot be the whiner in this discussion."

A session is in session.
It watches the mountains of rock-hard farce-ships,
and doors break.

They break even.
I am living.
I bake caterers —
and for the right cause, I bend
without a rhyme.

Okay, I'll sweep the floors.
Ah, yes, of course!
I'll bring you hope,
and hope for you to see me feel.
I'll deal.
It'll look so real,
mean a great deal,
A man who copes is a man who is probably made
of steel, but also cotton.
And I do feel,
But not for me.

I ask dumb questions and attend lectures,
I make assertions so as to make honorable
mentions. I wry 'cause I get
bored,
I lie 'cause I can't die.
I lie only because I am to myself —
a man.
A damned character of choice.
Steadfast.
A rock-hard farce-ship.
It may drown, and I may frown,
and in No One's Land,
I am the crown!
I bring fast and orderly fashions,
I make lions out of meat,
And I'm so sweet —

that you just can't.
I can't.
I just can't with all these —
Can't!

Nothing — is all that it was supposed to be about.

Tale

A cross.
A wonder-tour which is the brute's dream.
Safely disconnect.
A tidal wave files through, sitting behind a desk
which is higher than its seats –
A remark.
Laughter.
Leaving body marks unattended.
Viler.
This rotten skin shows itself plenty.
Heads turn.
Pores of sorrow visit from a window.

A shadow, if only I could catch it mid-flight.
Functioning within my human right, a brainstorm
is menacing the trenches.
A human light – the monster of the sea, becomes
the maid's honor, which is but a man.

Behaving monstrously.
Taking the dog's king out for a walk.
Into one's own, a waste of time and peace grows
gold.
Godly tanks in the middle of autumn come take
you under their wing, imbuing
you with swift destiny –
Bad dreams, sink, retrieve the simple things, repeat.

Times change when you die.
It is worth the wait, then you break you and take your misery in my holier arms.

Dreary, dare none.
Back sweat, sense none.
Sweat drops down on a parachute with a destination –
Blinding lights from all directions, down that milky way of propaganda,
Rapid, feisty – they are here to break your tits, to stand on your toes and shake those thighs.

Are you apologizing?
Fill in the spaces with filth, blood and disgust.
Feels good to mean nothing at someone's final moment of choice.
Hold now, keep your face down, under the metal, on this day of aging and silent remorse.
No.
No one is waiting for the again to recur.
And the again does do its common thing.
A day of reckoning pisses the people off,
raises pleas to their call, to be their rock, which is a grenade.
I will play dead.
Play dead, whore, play dead.

Punches come through as I speak to the whatever God.

Remember what was done to you! What you had to endure.
Pack a tile and heart-wrenching gut-stress. Keep some ink in your drawer.
Open it. It is still there – the stench of a full belly; a semi-functional party of half -bald and practically incapable individuals, with their nasty darkening meat for
skin, for art.

It befits you, with your blackened nails and innate argon.
A statue is called Paris, with the –
Get down.

A fool for you, I cry with my all which is just a man, filled to the brink with animosity, having commenced in a dream.
This happened. My perilous state passed by. Too you and too anyone else to admit that I needed life, so can
someone come and play my strings?

No warning was given.
No one came to sign me off as I cringed from my life.
Leftover meat – is me.
Will I stay here?
Do I even have a choice?
A new product.

A new side-boob.
Here is a spicy sauce to fuck with you.
Bring me home, bring me back.

Why call the gods for aid, from the depths of a dream, where my lover is slain and my voice is thin? Swing as hard as you can, homeboy. Come on in
without a warning. Without a sign.
I want it alive and pain is living.
My pants fell down, and the wings of an eagle cried out.

I want your love, ads and small marketplaces.
I want affairs, but not the usual stuff
but the curable kind, where I can go back to a prison of my own choice if push ever comes to shove.

Be not a man of your word.

Boo, man, boo.
Take me in and dread with me.

This was the tale of how tile, sorrow and graphic design came into practice.

Danny Krivosh

Space Echo

Something dark is coming.
A brand new sky – born to die.
Dim and dumb, undone by an echo.

No, no one, no one is, no one is even here,
and no one cares to remember –
Remember that one day in June?

We'll pack up and go,
or how about we celebrate excuses?
We'll get some food, put on a tune.
Dance as we would, not as we should.
Desires and vague little scripts in the fire.
For half a thought – a penny, a thought out loud, a
cube or a crypt.

Proof they never existed in the first place –
Disqualified.
The points go to –
just disasters in disguise,
and each star is sick of looking at a teary blue
world –
the same tedious blue view.

Calmly fleeing the scene and darker the thought
becomes.

The still, blue, young night will set the stage no more.
Shrill sounds to make sure the audience is still awake.

What distance lies between us? I ask – nay, cry
– nay. Beg! for Heaven's sake –
Crack open the door and see how we're all gone,
just gone to Hell on a silver platter to behold.

I can't help but breathe your disgusting cigarettes,
you shady human silhouettes, huffing, puffing,
Holding butts,
Shaking butts,
Loving lots,
I am getting there, I swear.
I will now become what I have never dared, or never wanted?

No, no one, no one cares.
No one cares to remember.
I'll pop right up and out of their silver-lined gazettes, their salads, their spoonful and dressings all over,
and dresses, and fingers –
Forced to scroll down through all the settings and unveil a hidden button to
drool on.

Radio in, radio out, there is no sound.
I have nothing and am to no one.
Relax, it's time to float.
Float left,
and all that's left is this goddamn smell of fucking crap.
Burned memories...
All I'm left is this – is this mine?
It's all we are – take it.
It's all I am.
Time to float.
Let's carry on with nothing on top of all of our yesterdays, burning all alike in incredible fury to be felt by no one.
Sink, drink, drown, retreat, restart, get to know another world, another one to try on for size.
The river stiffens. A star becomes the silent reproach of a million tear-stained eyes.

Baker Street

Part I

The above has collapsed on the outside.
It's all over the news, which means only one thing
– it will be included in all editions to come.
They say that the sky had done found its match, reached its limits and shit.
Upon re-entering anew, a feeble theme took charge, and the grey was to be kept deep in a hole.
In retrospect, the above was fine; never a black-suit-wearer, even if it seemed that way to some…
"I am so sorry for the intrusion, but—", said the color pallet-colored Dredd to the wet earth cold dry.

"Care to join us? We are missing a person on our team –
we are spreading the hate, which to this date is the very reason for our fine existence.
We stand tall, suspecting it was the short black earth that took the evergreens from us.
Any given mortal can now exasperate, believe in whatever, given that the direct light of opportunity (a storm is coming from way under) saves their skin and bone for all eternities, and iterations of it to come."

I personally took the life out of the sun in a fit of rage, and waged an entire life against its burning wisdom –
which are but walls…
Traded the four of them for a queen and a multilayered understanding of chrome hardware, but –
No one ever cares anymore what people do or don't –
All they ever care about is spending their hard-earned money on questioning the god of no one, and those circle around the Earth's motives. (BO-RING!)
Action calls for me, and I do respond.
"Gather around and join me in chanting: Why, o treacherous earth, why?"
Narrowed it down to a handful of words the other day, taking it with a friend to go.

I told him I bid against everything including the defamatory nature of our party, that there is an awakening bomb deployed at my feet, and all he did was ask me to leave.
A real friend… asking me if I'm up for grabs! (A real buffoon.)
By the end of the night, he held me by the stiff one, and we chrome-hardwared for a while there.
He loved how belittled and confused I got, and I did become one of the richest people to fall off the earth with empty pockets, but so what?

I was under me, I was all.
A smile, a church, a sky that was all over yet never, that shat all over me like I deserved.
"I say! Put that cunt on the stand and break its legs. He—
He looks tastefully guilty...
Too pretty, that's for sure! And where was I?
Oh yeah.

Part II

Rape him right then and there, straight back into his chair, and do tell him I love him.
Break that miserable chair of a man, and see what makes him."
Hector awakened in a wet bed covered with perspiration.
"It has to be it. It is finally it for me."
It took him a solid minute to get up, fully grasp the gravity of his situation, and take himself to go.
"I'm getting out of here."
He was right in taking to the outside, to the public' eye.
The celebration had commenced, and he was not safe anymore, being a public figure.
Naturally, a man of his status would attract some heat.
Major players such as himself took to the grin in front of a crowd that dared not to chant – no, not anymore.
Those were the days post-Baker Street's demise.

A spectacle of burning lives under a hood of something short of a miracle was establishing itself.
Hector was still alive then, even on the day that followed the celebration.
Those were THE days, albeit melodious dream sequences and harmonious activities were straight-up overruled.
Anything Heaven-made became outlawed.
It was dire, no doubt.

The days pre-Baker Street were a gift thrown away, never to return.
But –
we were set not to accept our miserable fate as it got bombarded upon us by the gruesome ideals – World Leaders (great name for a band).
There was a sense of abandonment, and each day was followed by another one just like it – no… worse.
All peoples remained in a broken state, while newcomers paid no mind to what mattered and joined the cause.
They became 'The New Ones', and they fought alright.
They had not a mind of their own – of that I'm quite sure,
For if they had, they would never have meddled with this shit, perhaps made better life decisions, lived, grieved over a past well-lived, but no –

Now they are to be taken care of – such a hassle, such morons, buffoons, murderers!

Hector got up, went for a quick shower, after which he took to the outside.
He slammed the door behind him and reached for the keys, but –
empty pocket!
Hector grabbed the handle again, so as to re-enter –
"No, Hector –
you are your keys."
Hector became bewildered.
He took a leap back and dropped down the stairs, all the way down to the lobby.
"No – Hector… do not waste your talents…"
Hail Hector the believer! The deliverer!
(Drink this.)

Hector's eyes were displaying insecurity. Lips? Skewed.
He reluctantly listened from a position that matched his grand stature, suddenly standing up on the stage and being the center of attention, but the chanting of his first name grew less and less desirable to the ears by the second.
"No. Umm-hmm. No – Hector—"
Hector looked up, looking for his keys in his right pocket which was the sky. He then inserted his inquiring fingers into his pockets but to no avail,

and all the while his skewed lips were centered at no one in particular.
Surprise, surprise! Nothing in either pocket again.
Agitated, Hector climbed the stairs and re-entered the apartment looking for the damn keys.
Oh dear. Hector entered too hastily, and hurt his elbow on the way in.
'Stupid, stupid Hector.'
Nothing is ever broken, Hector.
"Put on your magic cloak, son –
Choke on this here medicine, son –
you are feeding now, and feeling it now, right? Son?!"
Burn, son – you won't even feel it.
Trust your masters.

Part III

Hector's face sure appears pale, and look! He is already becoming less!
So does the ceiling of my one true happiness, Hector thought to himself, never murmuring a sound.
Less….
"Play less –
strip and confess –
pay less –
be right less, and as for your dirty underwear –
I am all but incomplete.
I do, undo, and redo wives.

That's me :P
Go and cum, and let me follow you."
The faucet dripped as it got personified by a Word document.
It turned with intent into the format .doc so as to nauseate the mind,
and the image that flew by the converters caressed the empty broken skies of the now,
carving the skin of a cloud with false goodbyes –
they're still up, by the way.
Some of them are staying the night with us.
Hope you don't mind.
Shut up!
Sit upright!
Air-tight, just right, wait for me for an hour and a half on this shrinking bubble you call your dream bed.
A screw-up was here.
"I'm still here! Tilting endlessly!"

Part IV

Cold is the side of the bed where Mr. Reed used to lie.
I am the heavenly between, your narrator – a long-lost son carried away by the deep.
I used to keep him company.
Since then, I turned incapable of praying right, so instead I cry endlessly for a son.
With him, I'll wet the bed (with him), and then I'll

give him some advice, 'cause that's how the song goes.
The song must ALWAYS remain the same, right?!

"Well! You're a long way from dying, Mrs. Reed!" yelled Hector at the poor woman who was less.
"It's Ms. Reed–" she corrected him, having lost her mind and husband to the likes of him.
She never cared about nor condoned past atrocities.
She tabled to the cause, she -
was actually about to die herself.
"I can't be of much help, but at least I'm something to a certain somebody. Of that, I'm sure!"
Young and tried, sad and tired Ms. Reed was about to go under the Earth.
She was a hundred words, but her mouth kept failing on her every chance she had to mouth 'yes'.
An always-late crate of something truly great got into an accident on that somewhat tragic day.
Baker Street was packed.
The thought How come I miss you already, after being gone for just a lifetime? was interrupted by the clash of two vehicles.
Ms. Reed hid underneath the table, listening to the atrocities happening outside.
Not exactly gone, but rather gotten and misread she began imagining lovers (dying)…
Well, they do cherish their coffee and burned meat, she thought.

Oh, but not together though! Never mix the two.
Oh, that would be ghastly for the taste buds.
The song must ALWAYS remain the same.
The misdemeanors are being carried out on the street –
but what if they come inside?
Guess I'll quickly ask for a check and leave, run for my life.
See you never, Ms. Reed!
And…
She just missed the queue – left to die by the crater on the side of the road.
She awoke to a light.
"Mrs. Reed, please call me Hector."
"It's Ms."
"Ms. Reed?"
"Ms. Reed indeed."
"Well then, what can I do you for?"
"I… uh, felt a chin under my tumor."
Right... she's the one with the tumor. I remember how she feels down there, Hector recalled with a smile to die for.
A boiling sector of dims and dumbs burning together as one, in laughter, came attacking Ms. Reed at once.
She asked if she could lie down.
What a coincidence, that's exactly what Hector willed!
"Oh, it burns quite bright, but I'll be alright,", Ms.

Reed lied, and went on: "Me! having the right to be calm. I suppose I choose to rather than have to!" The con doctor's music for a nurse, which was nothing but fake laughter, cast a spell on his new favorite patient, leading her straight into the man's arms.

Hector died rather happy, with a stupid grin on his stupid face, having not achieved his dream of falling without spilling, but who gives a shit? He went out knowing that the light that had cast its shadow on the earth once or twice before had a somewhat familiar hue to the color pallet called dread, which stains the skies nowadays.

Call Me Not

'Tis no time to be poetic.
Efforts are
endlessly earthly.
That should be the title of my emblem –
beginning my poem.
Let my thoughts conceal a beautiful face
With an abhorred breath.
Let mama darkness be there to its –
Let me suck it, babe.
And in your thoughts, I will behave,
like a little girl with a pretentious smile.
A horrendous deed.
Can you catch your breath?
Da-dooh, da-dee,
Duh-dum.
Sir Death has come.

I wanted that love.
I still remember how cute,
how cuddly in wintertime,
how soft and miserable –
a girl's cheeks are caressed...
When no one sees –
she's sliced to bits.

From whence she came,
from thin to unseen,

I told her: "Come hither, girl, come to Papa –
come and sit here,
right at this moment."
Then I told her to steer clear: "You hear?
You dumb witch, I'mma take what you never had!"
Not really.
Not ever really.
From this forever on, she never dared to
cling to another stone,
step anywhere near,
I hear, yes, I hear – I miss you.
You who was,
you who will never be.
Whis – whiskey – whiskers, milky tits and pain.
Come, come and sit here.
She might have gone further ahead than I wanted
her to go.
I miss you – don't come back.
She might in fact be dead as far as I know.
I want you
to not come back
because I hate
that I miss
you –
consider how we were all compared
to all great suffering made
by fuzzy little good cat –
God's creations with no desire to be nicknamed.

Brown to Brown

Suffering
by and by,
by and nigh,
through and through,
until this very moment,
just as true,
or perhaps it is a lie.
But along with you,
I rot in disdain of my duplicity.
It is but freshly-rotten skin.
You know, and, and then in fact,
I make linen out of text,
so I could hold you right here with me for eternity.
Right where you began loving me.
Right then.
Again and again.
Hell!
Her daughter knows it all too well.
To conceal is but to feel – is.
We've gone on writer's strike.
Damn it all – all be damned.
For eternity's sake –
Fuck!

A mother who hadn't had a name.
What does she have?
Not me, that's for sure.
Her daughter would not come home either.
Come – come.
A nickname –

They, they, is plural.
Clenching those darling teeth to –
I? I?
It grasped.
Her cute little feet bumped
Hard on the window pane.
It was all she could do –
That.
That she bumped her head right into that –
sight of blood and disgust in human kindness.
Not so kind.
Not the right kind either.
So charmingly disgusted,
limbs jointed against a window
Pain is all I'm able to –
Hey!
I? I?
I hope that you are –
well & tidy.
Underwear

Dripping blood.
Enthusiasm?
I will not.
Are not I?
Call me not.
I beg that you are
pardoned at the sight of some good food.
Even that tickled the wrong way.
A perfect pussy.

Brown to Brown

A cold-hearted ass.
Transitions from one self into the next.
No hiccups.
No backslides.
A past that was never but –
she was cute, wasn't she?
I was the worst that ever happened –
to her,
and to her girl that's trapped under still.
To her, to you, just about anyone here is –
invited to my gathering!
We'll have a ball.
A real fucking ball.
She will not be measured any longer!
Says who?
Leave her be?
"Call her not."

Nor will she be a mother, now –
Call her not.
Call her not.
A mother is not a mother.
And I will from this forever on
be a single loner in my private sector.
Aeroplanes reach through outer space to come and
–
"Get him!"
Get me.
Let that be my punishment for
what I've –

Danny Krivosh

To have to live without.
Yes. you are, yes, and yet
I'm a loser.
A coward,
sucker-punched by his own teeth.
Commit suicide straight away.
Call me not.
Call Now 1-800.
Babe, please.
Let that be all.
Let me carry this for us.
This alone – let that be all.
I'll marry this and this alone,
are you alone, by any chance?
She had no idea what was coming next.

Poor little...
Poor pure little curl of fast and nasty circumstance.
Girl, you've stomped on your own head –
Believe me.
You've cut your own goddamn skin.
You're dripping,
from within?
Your baby that could never –
try not to climb out and see.
Aware is all I am of all my sins.
The belly rubs.
O, my sins,
for all you were –
They were.

Circle round creation for just a minute.
Just for a minute, babe –
Come nearer.
Come fear.
Please ignore me.
Please be still.

Shadow on the Hill

Part I: Day

It's wind.
Kind to my soft milk,
it's weird – not a poem.
In living a life of triumph, lifetimes into misery,
Will stems from o's and zeroes.
Form establishes logic by turning its shape, onto
the sound of silence.
From series of one-to-ones, it
Breathes,
catches the lamp's halo
which is thin, barely seen through the loud evening
mist.

Load.
Heavy.
Be not revered, but bereaved, shattered.
Watered – mouth.
Be but beside a background of your choice.
No one ever wants to make time for anything, so
the eaves of nature abide,
hint at the landslide and ride down that milky way.
Slide…
Eventually, nature does what it must do best
– hide…
As such, advancements make way for the even veil
of the golden duress.

The duchess tastes –
Bitter, thank you, with a hint of snow.

Part II: Night

Felt up my pillow.
It is not unlike the wallpaper, which answers to none.
It calls itself 'psychosis' tonight, and to the chest of woe all of my worries go,
fleeing to be out in the open –
Frills like the emptiness of paying it forward.
Sure… I'll take forth a second time, on me. On –
Three.
Pay a visit to the toolshed of your choice and snail back to me –
Whole! You shall be, with a dish titled 'so-and-so' tied to thy name.
Whole…
Shit hole.
I take it that I left there…
A gorgeous let-on and an assuming face merged with through the mist.
They are together in this.
They don't need me…
I hang up.
Politely.

Part III: Eternity

A hard-on by this here pane, and an uneven slice of sanctity on the other.
Reduced, redacted,
Choice!
And like dice, devoid of chance or agency,
a state of urgency always takes the poor by the leg.
I hide from the shadow of this ugly yet oh-so-inviting yellow wallpaper.
It chose me, but I am alone with the thing called misery.
I retire to his place where one can call a shower a tiny little prison.
It pertains to the belly of the beast -- our 'light' in its heart of darkness,
our time to remember (on) the hills,
a secular number within our hearts' lost thoughts.
Light's full belly is indeed sound, and with its sullen stare it repays past events in the shape of untold memories.
Oh, how it eighty-sixes the animals portrayed on the silver screen, then wears them
for a hat.
Money!
Spend eternity in here,
in this shit hole with me.
With you on a hill I forget it all.
Hell!
Eternity must always prevail.
I welcome you all.

Part IV: Force of Nature

Scalded the back of my hand with your palm of smelly sweat and glue…
Sweet tiring mother of Just, you never stop – do you?
A ghost.
A ghastly old town, tarnished by misspellings of 'supernova' –
released to a day quota –
In order to serve, you must be brave enough to peep through this closed door, even if my darkness meets yours in this beat,
even when a heavy hiss drops aloud upon us –
comes heavy with a darkening mood and a shadow that disallows lids.

I want to be left alone for just a silly minute –
no company to behold nor form to uphold.
If models were alive today, they'd only be allowed to starve and claim they
had the right to their posters all along,
to have their fill which is to pour, harm, instill the poor with dreams.
Creepy I's that seem to have been following them around ever since.
They stand heavily guarded by the corridor of my dream, hand-tight.
Its atmosphere?
Black and white with ice cubes on repeat.
We are at the crypt upon our re-entry.

A saying always brings a dish best served cold,
carried by the puffy arms of tradition.
It is the land of misdirection; in its direction I must follow.
Willow is my form.
Pillow to be the stage name.
Albeit nurturing, nature is a desolated mistress to some
Perversions.
On this memory hill, I breathe but am otherwise still, as well as on my doorstep,
But the spiders –
They drop a pretty penny like a stone crest at my tuned feet.
I can sense the warmth of aged milk as I make way to the monster of the sea,
and she does appear.
She swings at me.
Yes, I do consent to a life of besiegement on this dying folly of a scorched earth.
You may conduct your interview and run your fingers on my sprawling spider body.
Let yourself in as you or anybody,
allow blasts from the past to regroup as beads –
then
carry them around.
Force a visit down Washed-Up Lane – comfortable and conveying.
Perhaps you are the kind who stumbles alone –
unbeguiled, unassuming,

frightful at the very sight of anything new.
The guns come a-blazing, and you hide from the one God that hunted your
dreams and left in a rush.

Part V: Cellular Communication

It is when two strings find each other that agency may pick one to imbue
with attention out of the bunch,
attack with confidence and dedication, and shoot straight to the heart of livelihood.
Here, in this humble store which made headlines last Thursday by becoming a
hot target,
a distress call is heard, and the firearm is loaded, getting cold.
The carrier came a long way from shooting, brooding, bearing, forbearing.
Caring…
Now he spends a little sentence of a lifetime in this prison made of crayon.
He is made to believe he is unattractive.
They call him inattentive, but he is always there, lurking, hiding with his hand made of sand.

Since the dying of the ages, a premise landed on this here Earth and kept on
booting pathetically.

The ground shook with moans, and mountains
rocked the humble store.
Fire.
The line became a blur, and as such – none of his
concern.
Behind a wall of segregation, he swore to keep his
family sane.
But an idiot should not swear…

At the crypt's tear and wear,
the dying age was being cast like a wallpaper for
him to admire.
He kept at large and stayed out of trouble, but the
wallpaper –
Premises were loaded onto a truck and handed out
as laden pamphlets to every passerby.
It only took 'one' for the effort to raise the earth, to
meet a life partner.
They were made to adhere to the home-lender's
busy schedule,
and all the while drown the blasphemous in a river
of emotion.
Broken mirrors, distractions and delicate poetics
were to be his children.
'Confusion' the bus came for us,
to take us under its wig –
it turned up from around the corner and cast its
phallic shadow on the poet's
toxic masculinity of a mountain.

"Sweet, sweet air of broken silence," the pillow whispered to the wind,
and the bourgeoise laughed their fat asses off, until they fell long and hard from the balcony of our home –
our shower where we become versions unmatched.
I am to run down this here hill and come out on the other side unharmed,
tuned down a half a step in any direction.

Part VI: The Couple

A deaf service maiden smirked at me.
Names got exchanged.
She laid down the laden pamphlet and asked me if I liked Mayhem.
I asked her if it was a band or some idea she'd had in store for years.
She scolded me, told me how she'd waited on me and on her chance to forgive,
while Hell –
We are arriving at 'eve-dropping inner-section' – so sayeth the deliverer, and
the bus comes to a stop.
Do not forget your luggage.
Carry on.
Hell came a-bursting, and this time I fell along with the bourgeoisie.
Security caught me smiling by surprise, while I surmised with a cigarette at hand.
In a timed yet fashionable manner,

I gave a notion.
And with a swift motion,
I made a crack at it, and,
Oh…
My dream fingers!
My aspirations got denied by a call that never went nor came through.
You may never know,
and so it is to happen.
The winds, the cracks and the hooligans made the apparatus of our hearts run out of coal.
The minutes of our plan, as well as that rigid wallpaper panned and dried out.
I became a cellular version of the teachings I withheld.

Part VII: Fire

At last, and at the very least, there fell a final nocturnal episode which meant
inventions, creations, as well as dumb conventions.
We took two steps back to the very early days.
Hopelessly varied; please untie me.
They were good.
The cave was even better, for in it we found fire.
No one interrupted us, and we took care of ourselves.
We were to be the only two shadows in the entire cave.
We turned deft –

right where the scar would have met a face instead
of a grin.

A line re-entered the banter of two flames
conversing, dancing, allowing,
complying, compiling, and the era of trial and
terror thus began.
Not much of a man,
is it?
Did you?
Have you –
had a man in your life?
Held a snowman to the earthly ground and cried
out in vain as it disintegrated?
Atoned or attended ceremonies of…
well…
Pain?
I am so, so sorry.
Do not cry.
You keep watering your mouth as needed, and the
juices keep on flowing.
Must be ready, ugh.
Wait!
On me with nothing fancy, accept my apology.
Three!
Go to bed, dear security – you're drunk.
You could have built a frameless frame, boneless
from scratch, but did you?
Do not keep safe and rigid like 'Psychosis'.
You are your own.

Go to bed!
Knight, Knight,
K-nights out.
K-nives out –
I never meant to do any harm, but the big
industrial world handed me a pillow so soft that I
just had to...
On that damned seventh day people seem to know
so well, the couple fell asleep smiling –
and their dreams fell short,
having had to succumb to their rightful masters.

Safe Bets

Drunk and alone.
The signs unravel heftily behind me.
The pavement rakes and moans.

Went and came over nature's body – a sweet
Salvatore,
then it was Winter that came and went.
Over.
My blood body.
Yours,
My name.

The bottle grew so heavy in the hand.
Am I proud of it?
My big, big boy, tried and true.
How could I ever go on without you suckling at my teat?

I'm gonna die soon, and so will you.
But until it is high time to sink so low as to rest in a final rocking chair –
Until then –
I will congratulate myself for having attempted to lead a life.

At night I am building a magical fortress in which -
purity of souls be damned, like virtues of a
natural-born killer –
something richer in confinement, all within the fine
limits of imagination.

Control means numbness.
Like a serial number, I am none without a whole,
but can survive anything, my boy.
My deflected defects are as that of a serial mother,
bouncing off hard plastered walls, where hardened
red-dyed lovers come to perish.
Well, confined in solidarity with both purity and
evil, the idea of romance keeps itself alive.
Behind closed doors where we are together –
Metal cries my name – long-forgotten,
mispronounced.
I await none, for I have none to bid my kinship, and
years go by.

I am pure release.
I'm distasteful –
you know my name, how disgraceful –
you've gotten to know the me on the brink. I am
self-importance –
Management of the will is my nocturnal
occupation and interest.

The top of my head is burning.
It does get warmer at night,

warmer in the bed of fire,
and I burst before it consumes –
I bid my fair will to insides' rot.
Whoever wants more of this will have to make do,
learn how to behave, accept less in return.
I confess – my boy keeps me silent.
"Bid farewell," it says,
"Let your voice cut loose in a worldful of litter."

Friend -- No Friend

He did everything so I'd remember him. He –
Gave me things –
and drugged my inner wings.
Friend – No friend.
Everything he said –
he said to sound true.
He said: "I'll let you live, I guess,"
but who am I to you?
Tablespoons, under tops.
Now riddle me this:
Has anyone ever told you
you lack conviction?
Identity?
Stupor.
We're –
Getting dumber
by the minute.
Getting higher –
by the Jesus.
We're getting dinner.
Any minute now.
"Good morning! Sunday morning to you!"
"What say you?"
"I've always loved you" –
"Is that so?"
"It is, yes...
but it isn't right."

I'm gonna start the fireplace – hope you don't mind,
you sweet – sweet-bottomed angel.
Tell me:
"You're miserable."
"Ugh… you're intolerable."
It's not what I asked, but do shut the fuck up,
and keep it shut for as long as you are able --
I'm blind,
and as I'm walking this Black Verse,
my thoughts undress and my ghosts disperse.
They cry in tears that rain down.
'cause you know –
once you let go,
Then it comes.
Then comes pain.
Then it shows in ages plenty.

Finally I realize something is the matter.
Finally I see -
Nothing is where I am.

Open House

Part I

Vaporized, I bicker, snicker and peek from within the hole you call earth.
Out of gin, I send you letters with my scent,
I break forth but only to wait.
Outspoken, re-awakened, conjoined to a wooden box with metal bars for names,
I cast my shadow and begin to listen.
I hear how shackles of woe ring true to a subdued heart, and the desire is thus numbing.
Then I sign by whichever you'd consider, and I's deliver us from ever lower.
Then it sinks even lower than that.
From deep syllable wombs, my human slave gets pulled and cast aside,
to be that whose wish befalls, in what dreams may come in a rising tide.
It has to be me but cannot be afraid to have to be,
so it can be half the saint instead of the making of a rising cause.
Angels –
Angels fall with a primary function.
You have to look into the eyes of a brand-new and quite empowering jewelry box.
You must get out, out of spite, out of a diamond but not without a heart.
Darkness cannot be reasoned with.

Herewith I call for treason, and as such, I am thus risen,
To make believe in appropriateness, and a darling speck of dust becomes a whine and causes a -lack of breath, as my bitches moan and drink.
I stir fresh air so I can have some coolness in my rising.
They have settled for less – I tell you.
They have waited long enough and distrusted higher winds.
Now they must accept me as their main proprietor.
Out of torpor, I am becoming less, and I press 'yes' for release.
You have awarded me with nickel wings, I say to them, and as I do,
The shieling in which I am currently occupying space gets narrower by the fleeting second.
It feels like it wants to collapse all over me.
Shelling is in order, and the tortoise stays on the brink.
Methinks of sea, of drink, of how the sand cries for help, begs to be seen, but I am only half the glass before getting rinsed. It is my father's arms I cannot escape –
My arms you cannot outrun because the mileage is too high on the meter called hope –
All-seeing.
No surprises there, and I just turn.
I turn still.

It is my pale skin that outweighs your heavy eyelids
as I turn to night.
A wave comes not out of spite, but at the sight of
some good old beast, hits the sea instead of the
tortoise and puts two keys in its belly.
My weak bones cannot cope under the heavy
crown, and so the other stages hit, and the beach
looks like it's bleeding.

I burst and drop to the ground – alive.
I pretend to be that ground before the earth's valid
disposition rationalizes with dirt and vapor.
Then I rise, too eagerly, too prematurely, and I am
captured and sold, and then it is done.
Such is the untold story of the non-traveling
salesman who once dared to visit the land of
corpses.
They were beneath him, but he never had a frame.
Such is the state of his pre-condition labeled
'humanity', and that denounced him,
made him quite neatly forgotten.
He got vague – you see, woke, tanked upon being
sent home from the field.
That was his life that was laid out in front of him,
Which was a box office disaster.
His is a product – you see,
a CD / DVD burner who waved goodbye as he
perished on an old woman's shelf.
He goes out of his way to head straight to town on
an old metal bird.

Peacefully but never peaceful, wave goodbye – you old perverted fashion bag of wrinkled time warp.
Greetings from brown foliage.
I own the village, and you are my kindly-lit folk people.
Please do not – have not a desire for my name.
All I ask is that you remain up to date with the wreckage, as it is discarded by the sides of the road by the date.
Have a quick taste of my buds.
But porn.
Have wishes, and upon them fall for just a minute there.
Hug time and beg for your dear life.
Wish – only do so on an old starry night.

Part II

The upholstery found a loaded heart to cling to and put its hand in, and it did fit like a glove.
I beseech and conceal nowadays.
I am rich.
I stay safe.
They caught me on-guard, unalarmed.
I am reliable, so trust my words.
I am unafraid, but I had to regroup and catch my breath before I could move out of myself –
for just a minute there.
Then I went back to get those, and Her Majesty sat up regardless of how she got melded, as if

there was a way for her to get back into nature.
A savage's blind eye can turn leprously black – you know.
From a place where protection isn't needed, I started to get my gatherings,
but wouldn't you know it –
Somehow I got sick all over my things, including my luggage and the no-longer-red carpet beneath my skeletal feet.
All whole and all at once, overwhelming life decisions had to come up like chasers and cloud my judgment.

First, I never stood a chance –
then I couldn't stand and I lost whatever actions may come.
I dreamt past seasons with weak arms, trying to put the wildfire out.
I almost claimed back what was mine but oh my Lord –
forget it.
I am rejoiced.
I, I, I have deactivated my father's panel, and weakened his shield for a lid.
Rain always wastes its mournful magic tears on my slanting figure of a person.
Forthwith, time sprung a sling, to rotate and spin –
So commenced the soothsayer, and at once, he got guided on how to be needed as an angel.

He had been crying everywhere and all at once
from birth, but not me.
Oh – he had such a heart,
having been a part of a singular family, abandoned
along the dead stars' way –
oh my fucking God – the stars…
When my father cried, they all retired like the
angels the people wished upon.
Dumbness ruled.
He started to stir.
He seemed possessed, calm and mediated.
He addressed the inner soul of the folk, which had
taken a toll, and the role was to be whole again.
And, and –
The earth shaketh, proactively and prominently
– eminently.
I am alive.
Specific – Don't touch me!

I'll do the touching.
I accidentally slipped, having no ground to step on.
Then you idiots cried out, but only to point out the
faults of my world's infrastructure.
What was the purpose, and where the hell have you
gone?
I need you still.
I'll be calm.
The masses hear my voice over the megaphone that
is sexuality, and that did it.
That is the sin that finally killed tradition.

Nothing escapes me.
I am good.
My dark city folk – how have you been and where are you returning from?
I want to taste you all, and can you at all see me without my father's figure guiding, leading, misleading, showering over me?
I speak to thee, hot sluts and life partners –
It is I who burned at your gates, you stupid (stupid) kings and queens.
I became unreachable behind the folk's locked gate of wisdom, and to each his own.
I am going.
I slit a stupid throat behind a wooden desk and marry a chair.
I am not trapped here –
unto a chain and collar.
Old friends –
I keep hesitating, resisting the urge of calling you on many a night,
and on afternoons for a nice coffee break.
We were great once, weren't we?
Not being able to retrieve a long-gone past is even worse than sitting alone in my awesome company.
I tear.
Have I changed? Tell me!
Whatever you do fascinates me.
Wherever your reach may end, you can always find me – kind souls.

Shit – is where you'll find me, and lie to me, where
my life can ultimately end you,
by a long shot, a slingshot.
A punch to the chin held tight with rage –
is where you will face me.
Deep silence falls and pulls a curtain on the endless
night.
So begins the era of leftover thought – me.
I control stillness now, and that is where I will
always find you.
You.
My beatific silent beasts of shredded remorse.
You.
A place that closely follows your definition of
'sleep' now has you by your good side.
In this 'sleep', I disclose yours truly.
My name did change over different mouths and
tones.
Even still, I come across you in many a direction as
one, and say:
All of your tongues I discard, and my name in each
will be 'underway is the toll', because
thinking of me should ever end with never feeling
alone.
I am emotional like that – you see.
I want to be made separate from the wrongs
capitalized by landlords and their ideals of right.
My agenda will not be consumed by bills,
disguising scars and a set of three silhouettes.

Part III

A compound might set you free, but also burden you with fears.
Watch me dance as Justice flees.
Are you alone?
Are your spirits gone from your eyes?
Can they hang with me?
Are you hopeless?
Never mind.
Your eyes are meant to see whatever eyesight I grant them through noise-music, but wait –
I'd rather not hold dominion over your country if I can just pull the carpet from underneath the
flesh and bones you call you.
Bring your sorry asses up to my offices and kneel upon my entering.
Only Deus the butler may walk out –
the rest of you must join me for dinner.
Me – be it your savior… I am getting out of here, getting my things and ending this captivity.
Me!
Now I am obliterated, completely reinvigorated and all-powerful in my wooden box with metal
bars for names and I am breathing heavily.
I will find a way out of here.
You will call me by my name, I will make sure of that.
As I exercise my power over the fragile seraphim, I am Being.
(Remembered.)

Brown to Brown

Aye, set the carpet for me.
I like red, thank you.
What do you mean you don't fucking recognize me?
I might not resemble my former self – sure, having a chunkier body and duck lips like a stupid-ass hoe, Sure – I have two golden teeth in the kisser, some hidden letters in the drawer and a visor to die for, but my promises are not to be accounted as cheap – I swear!
I am reliable.
Trust my words.
I am made different only by the giveaway of fake merchandise to the highest bidder,
and the products' relevancy is met with such currency that it gets relieved only to the highest respect.
I ask a somewhat fancy question with my mundane looks, put on an assuming face for you –
Call me pixelated and rotten, but –
the side quest goes on and you must come with me.
I must become stronger, prettier, dumber though richer.
I am no longer visually there, though I am in need of company, remembrance, respect.
I suck.
You missed me, but it so happens I care more about life than you babbling idiots with dying
features.
Meet me at the waterside.

An older, smarter, galvanized version of milk made famous by a stereophonic interval –
had the life beaten out of it with time-piercing punches.

Now the author is said to be prolific, because why not, right?
Within itself, as of itself, a relic of a specific past –
tell him to come and visit me in prison.
I will for his visit even though it costs way too much.
You can see it on my wrinkling face.
It costs perfume and a fortune to visit me nowadays, which is why you decide not to, and I shrink like the beast, instead of drinking the nectar of life like a god.
The TV moved an inch, but I am still your daddy's murmur when I get stiff –
I mean steep – drunk on anger.
I mean Jäger.
Love me some juice and some cheap black boots to fall on, lick, cry…
Shoot me.
I am at that mall in this video, producing a syllable, carrying out sins over my tortoise back for company – that is ammo.
I am a naked hot gun of pure decision and tentative release.
I shoot long and far, far ahead, and my smoke gets hard.

Brown to Brown

It has the smell of success and pudding.
I puddle.
Suck on it, my dear citizens of the simple earth
– suck on those tits and taste the dying fruit that
comes with aging.
Come bearing my nude pics in your basket of
choice, and add grapes of wrath to go along with
rot.
Come dressed fancily.
Shaken – not stirred.
Call for me, and I will come like a magnet to your
metallic fabulousness, and a word per mouth
will speak volumes until there will be no more
water.
Nudity is restlessness.
It drips, drowns.
Fucks with your morning as well as your drooling
mouth, made to seem reliable and realistic like
your narrator –
Whatever realism means to you idiots can be
played back in some sense of reverse.
I am of no concern to anyone who sees me for
what I truly am – anything less than hard conflict.
The angel is omniscient, a passed-on tradition,
word for word, mouth over mouth, scaring
idiots and lesbians since the very beginning – the
dawn of occasion and release.
There is nothing you can do but protect your kids
from my life's work – your efforts are futile.
Fucking with your beliefs is my expertise.

I am quirky like that, like a dirty bag of seed.
(I weigh as much.)
I own the greatest stories ever lived, and you and
your many centuries of towel-hiding in locker
rooms will have to make room for my greatness.
Hate me now?
I did give you sweatpants and pink nipples to drool
on, so respect me, goddamn it!
That's my name.
Those sad tricks might hide you now, but I am
coming, foreseeing – that is my promise.
I will be forever hiding in watch of you, having the
rights to your gown, to control you, whore you.
I have grown as the protector of this realm. I know
this much and more.
I am sorry, but I know you well.
I am your privacy as well as your number.
Call me.
Here is the emergency line where you can always
reach me.
Call me your distress call.
I beat myself to your pathetic reel drum.
Tell me –
that I look stupid-sexy in my red-colored shiny
armor,
that you cannot resist my smoking hot bod
underneath which lie invisible scars.
Say none of that if time is an issue for you.
Where we are is the brink, and through filth (ink),
dear brethren and sistren, I drink your thoughts

and marinade your meat.
Some wishes are too deep to be sent to Hell – what you may refer to as a well where you drop a coin for good measure and all is swell.
It's a good thing I can breathe underwater.
I manage to gather your prayers and catch them mid-air, respond to you with a touch of hunger.
Time does not slow down when I empty my cartridge over your photo album you call 'life', and memories remain on paper, stick, as I re-enter them mid-flight, adjust, sit back and kill.
Now the unprotected city you call 'Mayhem' enters my shop, window-shopping for butt sex.
This time, I will be the iron.
Watch my bleeding corpse of the man you see in me melt...
Have my favorite version of my name written in your lingo.
My open house is now ready for new visitors.
You are all invited to stand in line and wait, await, waste your time and go back to your kennels.
Those who were lucky enough to put their faith in me at the very beginning may enter –
My clique.
You were with me, and you will get your chance to breathe the same air as I,
as I embark on a new endeavor, to attach a new kernel to a beast with astonishing technique.
Join me, so sayeth the landlord.

Another trial-and-error journey miserably titled 'self-discovery' is upon us.
Oh, you're still here?
I thank you, first and foremost,
Now accompany Your Majesty – the one you love so admirably.
Raise a white flag of bravery if only to admire my hotness.
I do not belong with you, simple folk, except for when it is high time to differ,
and the snapshots go click, click, clickety fan, and it hurts – I admit to that at the very least.
I cried for months at once – once.
Purity is working for Puritans, but the experts who play along with it are missing the essence of
what makes the world round.
They always take and take instead of give.
Without them, though, my kingdom would seem empty, like a deserted land.
Allen-wrench for a belt suffocates the realm of emptiness that was once an open book.
Indeed, that strips away any fashionable tendencies and designs,
burns the pages like the ground for which I stood yet cannot stand any longer.
Burning is the sound of fire that calms the senses but takes no shape in its absence,
and for that one must be punished, for I am alone.
By being pushed to the sides of the road of no existence, one must ask –

should I exist at all?
And that, my dear simpletons,
is what I call a question.
Now shut up.
Centuries carry along centipedes to bug, to instill
the village with the idea of comfortability and
resort.
Just wave goodbyes, sweet sons of agonizing
mothers and penetrating father figures, and you
know you have done it right if you felt none of it.
Do – not ring the bell of my open house.
I won't answer. No – not any longer.

Waiters appear in front of me in a dream,
that's a good thing, because I would like to order a
meal of suffering,
but that which is a star
collides with my appetite and I cry like he did...
forlorn!
I spill all over me, and that too is a good thing.
I'm sensing skill from you incompetent idiots.
You want to wash my face,
and make me feel wholesome. I cherish thee.
White cloak-wearers, black seat-swearers – all in
all, can you imagine?
I need thee!!!
Whilst I do not necessarily believe in you, you are
my children,
and your sweet perfume does boggle the

senses like the lodged escapism of a stream called modernism,
and art cannot atone for you being blonde and stupid – your sins, not mine, stay away – don't fucking touch me!
Spin out of control, while you're safe and all.
Who, me? Yeah, I invented darkness.
Either steer clear of my smoking hot bod or ask for forgiveness.
Notwithstanding, time and time again, I take pills and spill all over the remains.
He who cares not about me will dig in and cower away, so that the resulting echo will scrap existence in an unfair millisecond –
Wrap the present in what can only be described as a silent but deadly note –
Punishable by death.

On the last day, the land became a desert.
Aye, it had been through so much drought, and now 'roaming' simply rules over the masses.
What is left are fair lads and empty discussions – no kings – just empty vessels.
Only utterly disastrous upskirts of people, half-seen yet more so missed in the background.
Step by step,
sip after sip.
Must.
We.
Change?

Brown to Brown

A text's draft needs syntaxing.
It cannot grow without a shell.
The tortoise is love even if it cannot tell a human from a pearl's heart,
and it certainly cannot distinguish between the efforts it took to balance the many streams of art.
Be not surprised if the wildfires catch you, due to your hubris, your enclosure being of a quartz quad.
Your city's walls echo the wailings of many a rhyme.
Ghetto playas and drunk fire fighters have gathered to chant –
but to whom?
In what fashion?
As the sun set, a sidestep was all the difference it took –
to make the winds of change break even, act out, hang down from the ceiling.
In my name, commercials were made, and those celebrated force, seasoned with raising.

A Single World

Please don't own me.
Please don't put me down to suckle and wear.
Don't cover me with rounds of plastic sheets and trap me here.
It's red and it's white – you're not fooling anyone.
Dear with me, tender lips.
Show me how loving you can be when no one seems to care about us.
Deem me in your favor and corrupt me with your hushed kisses.
Alas, I'm a human being.
Of course I don't want to know.
My words are just like ink, your ink.
An idiot for all to see – your goddamn idiot.
I have but idiot friends.
They surround me with their vicious circles.
Slutty dresses numb me down –
and wouldn't you know it –
they bring something with them to caress and fool from underneath.
They bring solicited intent,
little to no resemblance to what you may think of my beautiful mind.
Barred, crippled – yet not at all devoid of life.
Seasons, please don't put me down like that.
Understand there's no real choice in a single world but to be alive.

Be sure to close your eyes in a bedroom where bad men roam.
Cold hard stares, it shouldn't be so easy.
Evil – come hither, you heartless pig.
Bones inside a spinning vehicle.
Crispy crisp metal gates, crashing down on endless turf in what seems to be forever.
Creamy, tasty, isn't it?
For the love of God, it's still there, can't you hear it?
Don't take forever.
I admit – I am more than close already.
I have to admit to liking your true colors upon finding them out.
Now, haunting your tilted drapes like a bitch, I watch through bleeding eyes and see exactly what you're hiding.
It's a sign of me, on top of which you've pinned notes to cover your tracks.
Made it so it would hurt too.
I thank you.
I must.

Wheels

Teenage rockstar, Bay Harbor drunk.
She climbs on, 'hold my rear', and skates.
Oh, my dear.
Dreary fiend and hardcore friend.
She bites on this, and this attacks with a sudden
blow to the pray on tears.
Out of fear, she is exiled back to Wisdom Hall.
There she was made, befallen and detained, for the
rest of her father's care.
Be not a dame, but a damsel of distress, of chance
and collar in thy drawer.
Your socks may tell the story of many a fairytale,
but the shoe that once matched – now grows mold.

Braille the enclosed idea of getting ahead.
Bring me down and out-savor my naked body.
In it, I will cry 'help me father' and diminish.
Corpses may find me awake and pleasing.
I shall welcome them.
They will become my dreary brethren and sistren
and whole will become null,
since the day has always just begun.
I am tired, misrepresented, under-directed and
favorable, tolerable, miserable, horrible.
I dare say I cried, but can I become more than the
sum of my fears?

Sale, bail, stepped on my tail.
Fine, line, maybe divine.
Can't, won't, nor will I frown.
Sad clown, mystery gown.
Dark secrets wrapped in plastic sheets,
and hard lipstick smeared to merely seen...

Bye now, cruel sadness.
I will call me by some odd name and address the bridge's frail exit.
Here is mighty disorder –
there is some laughable wonder calling by the masses to a spirit, for help.
But is it help that comes our way, or some magic trick to withstand collision?
I pocket the change inserted in the cog machine and begin again.
There is more than meets the phone.
Eaves drop like ink on this A4.
Magic dicks carry fascists' sticks, and their women undress.
They are of service now.
They would have been their own victories, if they ever won.

The wheels have turned from mobility to mobilization, and Mozart shrieked.
How come the crown has more to offer than the thief?

Both carry forward with a sense of humility in
their formidability.

Tales, princes and queens, on boats on rivers.
On me, on your existence,
on your okayness, amateur hour is upon us.
The book is a bible, and the poem is Iliad.
The cousin is Eliyah, and the storm is awareness.
So self-centered that it wants credits for disasters it
did not partake in.
Bore, boredom and releases.
So freshly rotten, they leak nudes to the web –
and those, my friends, are a father's tools to club his
ascendants! Shoo, go on, get!
Take my word for it – no.
There was no LA, nor Sacramento –
just fire, everywhere I went.
Just terror, fear and gay clubs burned.
Just 'fuck all of you to save my gay ass' in every
hateful person I scarcely met.
They are meat in a grinder, pumped by meat and
stuffed with animal feces.
Animals' faces, tearing so that I enjoyed what
would otherwise go into some other asshole.
It is easy to live without care, principles,
municipals, rhetoric.
Just historic hysteria and rotting tomatoes on a
bridge do not make for a fast-selling experience.

Wake up on a morning without people,
look outside the window.
Open your full fridge and try to make a sandwich.
Kill yourself slowly, and as you do, smear your
blood and guts on a piece of old bread.
Let it sink through the hard cracks.
Those are your teeth biting into everything living
and asking to be caressed.
They cry because of whoever, and whoever is a
5-year-old popcorn-eating asshole in aisle 5.

Sorry,
but just kill yourself.

Not to be

I am all but prepared.
Untitled in my dazzling wants.
I did not know the whore I could turn to.
Geared up and alone in a puddle of my own,
awaiting judgment – foreskin.

The states' colors dried and fried, dyed, tied to no
avail with a nail to a timbre cock.
A wooden truck stop where people come to stick
and get stuck.
The mirror's seat is up.
Its promises are of –
piss, so as to not to be, no – not to date.
It burrows in that, and the upper hand falls,
to seal the deal and release the horny jailed inmate,
to set up shop where there was none – to sail into
dried-up territory.

Okay.
Hard to beat the state of perfection which is a
crying piss whore on a broken chair which is a
landmark for some.
I am not to be, haven't you heard?

Good day, prick.
Kind sir, a brick?

Pick me up and throw me onto another hit song on
the radio, to sing with, be with, sail alone
with.
Tuck that song between your easily-transmittable
disease-called-parents and solve the problem
that troubled so many of us for ages.

Not to burden anyone, I wish none,
can't wait nor want.
Am (to) not to be.
I count to 5, and then it is.

www.ingramcontent.com/pod-product-compliance
Lightning Source LLC
LaVergne TN
LVHW061526070526
838199LV00009B/385